THE BOOK OF INFINITE WISDOM

by

Mary Curtis

M.L.C. (Hom) Dip Hyp ISCH

The Key to SUCCESSFUL Living

Author of:

The Goldfish that Jumped

The Kingfisher that Rocked

The Heart and Soul of Success

Reflections of a Hummingbird

Dance of the Mosquito

Whispering Branches

---

marycurtishealer.co.uk

First published in the United Kingdom by
Mary Curtis August 2023

ISBN 978-0-9933734-2-8

Published by Mary Curtis

Contents

Testimonials

"What a read. About the book, it draws you in gently in a magical and childlike way but by the end you have been gifted an understanding of your whole life and found a new and beautiful way to live. Thank you, Mary".
Tony Smith, Life Partner

"Mary's wisdom deepens by the book. This is undoubtedly the most potent of the seven. A must read for those of you on an epic journey of self-development".
Peter Sanderson, #theprestonpoet

"This little story reminds us how one small slash of colour can brighten so many lives. We need reminding. We need constant reminders and here we have them. Reminders on how to appreciate life. Reminders on how to appreciate our abundance. Reminders of how to appreciate the joy in the now. Reminders that fighting change will prevent us from knowing the wonders that are to come. Most of all reminders on how to live, live in the now. This short story encourages us to grow in our spiritual life by opening our heart to others while blessing ourselves in the process. We all need these reminders. We all need this beautiful little story".
Susan Carruthers, Wise woman and healer

"Already the writer of six excellent books, Mary Curtis (the healer's healer) has surpassed herself with her seventh offering which I have been privileged to have an early view of. Her *Book of Infinite Wisdom* is a treasure trove for those seeking truth and self-identity, and I cannot recommend it highly enough. I won't go into it too deeply here, for I know that every reader will discover, as I did, the answers they are seeking in her beautifully constructed prose born, as it is from a lifetime of exploring what it is to be human. On a personal level, I have been honoured with Mary's friendship for many years now, and this latest offering of hers makes me prouder than ever that our paths crossed in this lifetime".
Stan Phillips, Poet

"This has been the perfect book to read after completing Reiki One and Two courses. The Reiki attunements that I received by Mary have made me much more aware of my own feelings. I was suddenly much more aware of both the small and large parcels of negative energy that I have been holding on to. Over my lifetime I am someone who has struggled to maintain my energy levels. This book has shone a clear light on the energy of gratitude that I have been missing all this time, which I can now tap into. This book has empowered me in a way that no other book ever has".
Dr E R Chare MA (Oxon) DPhil (Oxon)

"Mary's book is a gentle caress for the soul. Story and style is reminiscent of a childhood tales yet carries wisdom of the ages. Beautiful".
AK

"This book is amazing. I'm struggling for words. It has really resonated with me and certainly brought a tear to my eye at the end. Congratulations. This is your best book yet!"
Anjila Kanwar

"Mary's latest book 'Infinite Wisdom' is a book everyone should read. A book which everyone can relate to. Mary's exceptional standard of creative writing completely draws in the reader and it feels as though you are a character in the book. You can visualise, smell and taste every minute detail in the book. It's also a reminder to ourselves of the most important things in life; being at peace, being in nature and the power of truly appreciating the simplicity of life. We all have the ability to live our best lives with the gentle reminders from Mary through her characters, with a willingness to awaken our true selves to finding our own happiness, love, appreciation and self-worth".
Jacky Stuart

"Infinite Wisdom is a beautiful book beautifully written. From the moment I started reading I was transported into a world of learning. Learning about myself and how I can improve and how to

listen to others and the world around us. The attention to detail is wonderful. Love the intricate details of nature that is all around us if we find the time to look. A must read…".
***Sue Walle*r**

"I have known Mary for over twelve years, both as her client and as a dear friend. Reading this book I felt that she was telling the story of my own journey from victim of whatever life threw at me to reclaiming my power, but in the most amazing, unique way. This is a book which will resonate with everyone in different ways and may change life for the better. Please read it!!"
Esmee Grossman, Lifelong Learner

"Mary has done it again! What a truly brilliant book. *Infinite Wisdom* is reflective, moving, thought provoking and uplifting in equal measures. It really had me being present in my own life and considering just how full my personal cup was at the end of a busy week. Although I love what I do and am grateful and appreciative, I need to check in on myself a little more. Thank you, Mary, for bringing us another inspirational book".
Jeannette Pollard

"Lucky seven is a very special book. It shows us how we can break free from the shackles that have bounded us to what no longer serves us. It shows us that if we trust, have faith, come together, a better future awaits us. It is a beautiful, moving story of how we can live our best lives in a world full of obstacles, brought to life in an imaginative way which will touch the very depths of your soul.

I met Mary about 10 years ago just as I was going through my awakening. From the very first meeting, my life changed in profound ways. I was the stuck duck, the elephant, the crow, and one of my greatest lessons, learning to open the heart. My journey in life hasn't been an easy one and without the guidance of Mary, I don't know where would be today. This book is a beautiful reminder not to go back to the old ways – a new life awaits us if only we can trust and take that brave step into the unknown. Do what scares you and you will have no regrets. Thank you with all my heart for your guidance, wisdom and your love, all packaged as a gift to the world in this beautiful little story".

Angela Kilpatrick, The Holistic Coach

A Personal Note

Working in my professional capacity over the last twenty two years, I have had the joy of seeing clients change their lives for the better. Often one tiny change can create huge changes within their relationships, both personal and professional. My role is also to get them to recognise their need to commence a relationship with themselves.

Teaching people to become their own best friend and understanding why it's important to continually fill our cup, rather than repeatedly giving from an empty vessel is life-changing. Learning the importance of not burning ourselves out is often a huge revelation.

I first started writing this book whilst in my dear friends garden at Kurloon Retreat Centre, Pilling. From that day the inspiration simply flowed with ease, although it was November 2022, before I finally collated my hand written notes and began to type on my trusted laptop.

I was so moved and touched as each of the characters came to life. I recall actually seeing and hearing them in my mind's eye. It's truly been a pleasure to write and such a joy to research too.

Many of you will be aware of my love for the Hummingbird. It has been a power animal of mine for numerous years. I have so many gifts of beautiful Hummers all over the house. I treasure each and every one. Their essence is to bring joy to the world. Just as it is my passion to bring joy to those I work with.

It is my desire to visit Canada and see them in their natural habitat very soon. The thought of seeing them makes me incredibly excited and I know there will be many tears.

I truly hope this book has inspired and touched your heart and soul. Maybe it's lucky number seven for me? I have loved writing all my books, though this one is particularly favourable and deeply personal. It represents my inner journey from deep-rooted emotional pain to self-peace, acceptance and One-ness.

Sacred love and many sacred blessings

Mary x

Thank You

I am blessed to have a wonderful supportive family and some awesome, if not quirky friends. Thank you to each of my amazing children and especially my granddaughters. My parents have been my rocks over these many decades.

To Caroline W. and Caroline H.M. how truly blessed I am to have you in my life. Dearest kind Malcolm and Nicole Thorogood share great wisdom and deep friendship. My dear friends Rita and Keith provide me with a lovely hideaway when I need a break from life. Their garden is one of the most beautiful I have ever seen. To all at The Mirrie Dancer Café in St Annes, Tony, Tracy, Simon, Gary, Peter, Daphne, Jeannette, Jennifer, Jennie Baker, Alzbeta, Liz, Colin and Becky Clarke, Michelle, Stan, Ade, Lou and Emily, Eloise.

To Dickon. Without you this would not be possible. A million thank you's. Words are never enough.

To Angela for proofreading and her support, encouragement and thoughts going forward.

My beloved partner Tony is my rock. He's provided endless support, encouragement, integrity and guidance, done much of the proofreading and brought so much joy, wisdom and laughter. Tony you are my home. Thank you

Sacred love and blessings Mary x

Introduction

The lady of the sacred turquoise lake near the revered mountain came from a place of complete acceptance, pure love, harmony and balance. She had a magical air of connection around her, a deep abiding grace, a rare peace, a certain stillness and so much more. She had finally mastered the art of self-peace, self-love, acceptance, grace and One-ness. She was beautiful. She was radiant and at times it seemed there was such a bright light around her that she blended into the sunlight. When she smiled, it seemed the whole world brightened. Being in her presence was a sacred gift and a blessing.

Her life journey had taught her many things. Before her birth, she came from a place of infinite peace, connectedness, deep wisdom and complete acceptance of all things. She naturally assumed that all people would also be accepting and peaceful.

Little did she know that the word assume can be separated: ass-u-me. (To make an ass of you and me.) She was innocent, accepting and naïve. She felt a huge connection with her own self. Her heart. Her soul. Her One-ness. Her home. She wanted to feel a connection to everyone.

This is a story of her journey.

Chapter 1 - Connections

"Can you taste the sweetness of life?" asked the Hummingbird.

"How much love is there in your life?" asked the Elephant to the Hummingbird.

"You always seem so happy, content and blissful. You always have a smile on your face. You have a light-heart, always happy to see one of the other animals in the jungle and make time to greet them. You seem so light when you fly between the flowers and over the valleys. You seem to love being wherever you are, whether you are with friends or other hummingbirds, regardless of their size, colours or where they have come from originally. I always feel uplifted by your presence and I seem to smile without knowing why. The edges of my mouth simply curl upwards in your presence. My whole being softens.

It never seems to matter where you have been, or who you have been with. It doesn't matter if you're tired of flying by the end of the day. You always seem to be so contented, connected and graceful. I wish I could be more like you".

The Hummingbird smiled back at the Elephant. She had known him for many years. He was made to work hard daily pulling huge logs through the forest. He hated being used to pull down the very trees that were his beloved home. He was such a wise soul and was aware that there were so many other species dependent upon these many rare and sacred trees.

Tears began to form in her eyes, though she knew it was best to hold love for her huge beloved friend. Tears were necessary at times, though today felt different somehow. She wasn't sure why. She had learnt over many years of experience that it was better to remain in the present moment, to observe the emotion, acknowledge it, and yet not to become submerged, or reactive to it. She was all too aware of losing her power to emotions that could quickly get out of control.

She had watched others become reactive to their feelings and often live with deep pain and regret at a later date from that one particular angry moment, or unkind thing mentioned. The power of the loose tongue could certainly be dangerous at times.

Her thoughts shifted as she recalled his parents from many years ago. They were devoted to one another and although delighted when he made his way into the world, they knew when his arrival was announced to the rest of the jungle that he was soon to be tethered to a tree on a short rope.

He was now an adult and more than strong enough to break free of the rope, yet his captors left the rope around his ankle to remind him of his captivity. His deep, ingrained conditioning prevented him from *even trying to break free.*

She recalled the many nights she had hovered over him trying to console him when he couldn't break free as a youngster. But now he was fully grown. Yet he still didn't believe he had the strength to break away. Despite pulling huge logs daily, the rope around his ankle remained his *mental chain*? Could he really consider himself a *limitless being*? What if Hummer really was telling him the truth?

She was grateful for his friendship and recalled the immense pleasure it had given her to watch him grow. His parents had been relocated to another part of the jungle which often left him feeling sad, isolated and lonely.

It became normal for him to accept that he could never break free and he accepted his life without freedom. *And yet....intuitively something nagged deeply inside his soul.*

"How much love is there in your life?" he asked Hummer. He was aware she was thinking about other things.

"You always seem so happy, contented and seem to have boundless energy".

He feared love. His life seemed to be covered with a dark black cloud. And yet she seemed to see life through rose-coloured glasses, compared to this dark, heavy, oppressive mist which threatened to engulf him at times. Hummer answered honestly, knowing her answer may not be fully understood.

“How much love is in my life?” She paused for a while. He watched her as her eyes began to widen and her tiny wings beat even faster than normal. She did a backward loop which always made him smile.

“Oh my goodness. Well, I guess there is lots and lots of love and things to be grateful for. I awaken every day with a feeling of appreciation. I look forward to each and every sunrise. I love watching the colours rise over the mountain, the reds, the pinks, the yellows and the golds. They each touch my soul as they spread their lightness over the whole valley. The dawn colours are always so stunning. They awaken the earth and seem to kiss the valleys and the plains with splendid, golden light.

I listen to the sounds of the other birds and we smile and sing together with the new dawn. Of course none of us know what the day will bring. But, we choose to smile rather than be sad, or miserable. That’s our choice and our daily mantra. We sing to welcome the sun, the light and the warmth she brings. We appreciate the radiance of the sun warming our backs, our bodies and giving energy to our wings. The sun brings us together. Without her we would be in a cold darkness, without food and die. As we watch the sunset, we give great appreciation for another day, no matter what the day has brought to us. Death and change are the only two things that we can ever be sure of. The way we choose to respond to either is our personal choice”.

“But what have you got to smile about?” Elephant asked. Her reply was swift and effective.

“Well, the honey, the nectar and the pollen are always so delicious when I taste them. The flowers smile at me when I approach them. They never worry about sharing their bounty and simply allow much more to be produced. There’s plenty to share with the other birds, insects and creatures. We love to taste the sweetness of each individual flower. Even when I’m approaching the flowers, I feel as though their colours touch something deep within me, in my very being. It’s as though they are welcoming me into their arms. I particularly love to enter the heart of the rose, the inner rose. It’s a peaceful, abundant and beautiful place. Each touch my heart and my soul in their own unique way".

She paused for quite a while, lost in her own inner world, contemplating the amazing colours and the huge variety of stems, the different shaped petals and the sacred geometry that linked them all. She thought of the sounds that only the birds and insects could hear when the wind breathed upon their sacred petals.

Each of their shapes and sizes were unique. The orchids were so very different from one another and even though she couldn't feed from the ferns and the huge palms, she loved the variety of the differing green tones, hues and shades. They seemed to change daily. Was it the sunlight? Was it the light from the canopy through the other trees? She recalled how magnificent they looked under the light of the full moon. She breathed a breath of pure joy, deep abiding gratitude, connection and self-peace.

She became lost in her thoughts. She was distracted and fell into a deep, inner reflective place as she recounted all the dazzling variety of colours, fragrances and scents, the lightness of each and every petal, the beauty of nature, the incredible structure of the vast array of trees, palms and flowers. How could they grow from one simple, tiny seed, bulb or pod?

She smiled to herself as she imagined the raindrops falling over her beloved home. That was one of her favourite sounds. As the droplets touched each and every flower, palm, or leaf, the jungle sounded as though it had its own orchestra that had suddenly been awakened. A cacophony of musical wonder. It was like her own personal healing sound bath, which surrounded her from every angle, her own personal tubular bells. Every note resonated through her being, her heart and her soul.

The intense magic of watching one water droplet fall from one leaf to another, from one petal to the lower petals and the inner petals, too. How blessed she was to be able to hear with great intensity and feel such connection to it all with profound appreciation.

She loved witnessing the droplets forming puddles. They soon became tiny streams, which soon became bigger streams of life-giving fresh water. Little channels appeared wherever they could, following the pull of gravity that guided them downwards. Yet another beloved sound she loved to hear as the water forced its way down this sacred mountainside.

The waterfall was her absolute favourite place in the forest. She would try to explain frequently to her beloved friend the Elephant what it was like. She wished he could accompany her there one day, that she could witness his joy as he splashed carelessly in the river and the sacred pool below. She knew he would not be bothered by the other river creatures. He was so big that crocodiles would flee from him. She took solace knowing he was always safe, simply due to his incredible size. The thought of his full body being submerged and cooled by these incredible sacred waters filled her heart with joy. And yet...

Chapter 2 - The Potential of Freedom

Hummer's thoughts turned to sadness when she recalled how the two-leggeds had destroyed the lower valley. The birds could fly easily from the destructive metal creatures which cut through the trees with ease. All the animals that survived, looked with horror as their homes were ploughed down, destroyed, flattened and left abandoned. The Native American Indians always replanted seeds, trees and flowers whenever there was death.

She realised tears were forming in her eyes. With utmost care Elephant wiped them with his huge trunk, before they fell, as he always did. The unconditional love between the two friends was tangible. Many of the other forest creatures loved to see the Hummingbird and Elephant together. Witnessing their conversations always felt sacred, incredibly special and brought a warm, glowing feeling. The creatures all aimed for that loving kindness in their relationships.

This morning something was definitely different because for the first time he cried too. So big were his tears that Hummer could almost drown in them. He let them fall freely as sadness engulfed him. Was he feeling the pain of Mother Earth? Was he actually aware of her heart beat and her presence? He felt something stir in his heart, as though something had moved. He then felt as though something was opening.

More tears fell. Both he and Hummer knew something profound was happening. She flew in front of him so that she could see her beautiful reflection in his teary eyes. She hoped that he would begin to see his own beauty through her acknowledgement of her own beauty.

This was a sacred, magical moment as the silence of the mountain, the forest, the lake and Mother Earth touched his silent receiving heart. His heart was opening, seemingly clearing out the old hurts to make room for the new. But...what was the new?

Chapter 3 - Reflections

Hummer was silent. She held sacred space whilst allowing his tears to fall. Hummer's thoughts deepened. She was able to acknowledge her beauty and her size, tiny though she was.

"Can you taste the sweetness of life?" asked the Hummingbird inside his heart space.

She had asked him this question every day for many years. Today he actually seemed to hear her and felt her reply in his soul. Was he imagining it? Something was definitely different. Was he different? Was she different?

He often wondered if there would ever be colour and joy in his life. But could he welcome it? His life was a strict routine governed by the two-leggeds. That was all he had ever known. Surely it was impossible to welcome change? His mind raced as he actually considered the possibility for the very first time.

He missed his parents deeply and when he looked at his huge frame with his deep wrinkles he felt no one would, or could ever love him. With his huge eyes how could anyone really see him? How could anyone see into his sad soul? How could they love his huge legs and huge feet? How could he kiss with a truck? What a ridiculous thought.

He felt helpless and was so tired of these repeated thoughts which consumed his energy on a daily basis. He felt stuck. He felt sad. He merely existed and had no idea how to live more fully. Could he really welcome love into his life? Why was Hummer always so bright, loving and so full of life?

His sad tears stung him every day. But the tears in his heart left him broken and so full of grief that often he didn't even want to wake up. He felt he had a black cloud around him. Day after day it was the same old, same old. And yet...

He pondered change for the second time. He was certainly tired of living life in this way. Actually, he realised he was exhausted. He felt drained and understood that the 'Black Cloud' was killing at least a part of him. Could he really change? Could he force a smile for Hummer? Suddenly, he had a moment of utmost clarity. The choice was so simple. And...it was his choice to make. To allow the cloud to keep consuming his energy, or to take on board what Hummer had said and 'fake it 'til you make it'.

He tried to smile, forcing his huge mouth to open a little and then his cheeks followed and lifted. Within seconds he was laughing a huge belly laugh. The earth shook beneath him. The noise ricocheted through the trees, the palms, the ferns, the flowers and the whole valley. He stamped his feet, a sign of his determination that this was now his new way of being.

"Fake it 'til you make it," indeed he thought. He made a promise to himself that he would practise smiling daily. If he missed a day, he would get back to it the following day. Hummer had explained that it would soon become a habit and would then become a normal part of his everyday routine.

Suddenly, he realised that his whole body was shaking, as though he were shaking something off. The rope that had held him so tightly released from the tree that had held him since he was a baby elephant. He began to laugh – a deep, hearty laugh. Hummer sang with great joy. The other birds had already gathered around after hearing his laughter. The whole forest had suddenly become even more alive. Today was the day of rest for the humans, so today was literally becoming his day of freedom.

Hummer cried tears of joy. She felt she could literally pop with sheer delight. She did another backward loop.

"Follow me," she cried.

"I have something I want you to see".

She led him through the jungle. They smiled and greeted their fellow creatures. Others began to follow them through the thick canopy. Elephant stopped as they neared the waterfall. The noise scared him, though he trusted Hummer's words that all would be well. She motioned him on. He began once more to move his huge legs.

He let out a shriek of delight and surprise as they came upon the magnificent, sacred waterfall. The water descended from the great cliff into a pool of deep, swirling turquoise waters. The sight combined with the noise was so incredible his heart leapt.

Hummer guided him to the edge of the place that she had wanted to share with him for so long. She was elated. The cool water that splashed around him as he reached the waterfall brought such refreshment to his already hot, dry skin. What a wonderful feeling. The water soothed his parched skin and his whole body. He was so thrilled. He entered the deep pool. Soon his whole body was covered.

Suddenly he was swimming. How did he know he could swim if he'd never been here before? If he'd never swam before? The inner knowing within his body took over as he splashed and splashed in this magical place.

The sunlight shone through the water making it look like the most sparkly of diamonds. What a special, splendid moment this truly was. He had never seen fish before and watched in awe as they moved easily and effortlessly through the water. Frogs jumped into the pool and he was amazed to see their strange legs propel them through the water. Listening to their mating calls as they got louder and louder, he was in awe of it all. He was an innocent child witnessing a natural marvel for the very first time.

Dragonflies and butterflies danced over the surface and were so graceful as he stood in silence, gazing upon their magnificence. Many were mating. He watched in silence as two became one.

He loved the feeling of cool, sacred water covering his whole body. If only he had had the courage to listen to Hummer before today. There was no time for sadness. No time for regrets. He was here to honour these precious moments and the magic of this experience. He placed his head under the surface of the water and when he re-emerged he squirted water through his huge trunk to the other side of the pool. All the creatures laughed with him and each were touched to share his first moments in their beloved pool. It soon became a game as so many of the other creatures joined in the fun. The sound of their laughter echoed through the valley.

As Hummer hovered overhead, he ducked underneath the surface again and watched her tiny form through the water. This place was pure magic. It was bliss. Now he had no need to fake a smile as his whole body seemed to be smiling. Every single cell felt alive and vibrant. He had never felt such joy. He would remember these precious moments forever.

He breathed more deeply, breathing in this pure, absolute bliss. He felt whole, complete and at one with everything. *He had always felt safe when Hummer was around, now he could begin the process of feeling safe within himself. He could learn to trust himself more*. If only he'd listened to Hummer earlier. Hummer had mentioned that there was an Elephant Sanctuary near the waterfall. He'd trusted her once. Maybe, just maybe, he could trust her again. At this exact moment all he knew was that he could no longer return to a life of control, a life where he felt powerless and dead – at least in part.

"Can you welcome joy into your life?" she called to Elephant.

He didn't need to answer today as he smiled with genuine gratitude to his beloved friend. He had loved her for years, though now he appreciated her even more. *Now he understood when he listened to Hummer explain to the other creatures that there was a huge difference between merely loving someone and appreciating them, too.*

He vowed to remember gratitude and appreciation for this magical, marvellous day, these sacred, precious moments and he gave thanks to his beloved friend, Hummer. She had opened a window in his heart and soul. Now he knew he had to keep it open.

Appreciation was his new found key. That would be his daily focus, from dawn until dusk. His decision was made. He would trust her and allow her to show him the way to the Sanctuary.

Chapter 4 - Trusting the Power of Change

A beautiful sunset moth appeared. He rested at the side of them both. His wings were stunning as they caught the dawn sunlight. They shone with such vibrancy they both gasped in awe. It never ceased to amaze them that if he flew in the subdued light of the shadows, in the shade of the huge trees, his wings were far less remarkable. Without light, his true beauty could not be recognised.

Hummer knew that she too needed the light to shine. The light that shone through these magnificent trees brought light to feed the whole jungle, the trees and the ferns, not to mention each of the precious flowers allowing them to produce the sweetest nectar that gave her life-force. It allowed her to shine her unique divinity to the world. The sun gave warmth and brought the vast array of colours to this magical ecosystem.

The sunset moth explained that he and his family had found a new home in the next valley. They were sad to be leaving though he had intuited that it was their time to move on. He wished them both well and thanked them both for their incredible friendship and kindness over these many years. They all smiled to one another, knowing that change was inevitable. They hoped they would meet again in the future and trusted that if it was meant to be, it would happen.

The moth honoured his heart, too. He wondered if Crow would one day recognise his inner and outer beauty. Like Hummer, he knew that it wasn't for either of them to make him see the aspects of himself. Rather they were here to support and love him, to hold a sacred, loving space with absolute kindness from their pure hearts until he was ready.

He remembered Hummer flying over the Hopi Indian camp one night and listening to the wisdom they exchanged in their conversations around the campfires.

"There is a river flowing now very fast. It is so great and swift that there are those who will be afraid. They will try to hold on to the shore. They will feel they are torn apart and will suffer greatly.

Know the river has its destination. The elders say we must let go of the shore, push off into the middle of the river, keep our eyes open, and our heads above water. And I say, see who is in there with you and celebrate. At this time in history, we are to take nothing personally, least of all ourselves. For the moment that we do, our spiritual growth and journey comes to a halt.

The time for the lone wolf is over. Gather yourselves! Banish the word 'struggle' from your attitude and your vocabulary. All that we do now must be done in a sacred manner and in celebration".

The three creatures smiled and hugged each other in their own unique way due to their differences. They knew they would forever be a part of each other. They all knew they were a part of the whole and that they each had their unique place.

Chapter 5 - The Golden Thread

Hummer considered her life. She was grateful for the sun, the moon, the very air she breathed. She felt gratitude for her wings, their lightness and splendid, colourful designs that provided her speed, her ability to fly both backwards and forwards. She was grateful for all the flowers in the jungle that carried their sweet nectar providing her with the food she needed.

She had daily reminders showing her the sweetness of life itself. She also recognised that she brought colour to the jungle and its inhabitants. She was aware that she carried lightness and vibrancy to everything she touched daily. She felt her graceful power and knew she was appreciated everywhere she went. *She had learned to appreciate being appreciated, although it had certainly taken time to master that particular art.*

She hovered gently, close to where the butterflies were feeding upon some figs. She saw their beauty. Despite the differences in their size, shape and colours, they each had their own beauty. She listened as the beating of their wings kissed the morning sunshine. She watched as they devoured the sweet nectar whilst their tiny feet became covered in pollen. Life was all around her. Every moment a new bud was opening, new leaves were forming and butterflies were emerging from their chrysalises. She loved awakening to this magical world every day.

She thought of the days long ago when she saw that the other birds compared themselves to her. There was a time it made her feel sad. They seemed to feel inadequate besides her. And yet what should she do? Should she dim her light? Should she pull in her wings and hide herself? Should she stay far away in the jungle where few birds ventured? Should she really even consider not shining her light?

She shed a tear for her past self, for all the previous versions of herself. Long and hard she had battled with these thoughts. She had approached the Council of Hummingbird Elders who assured her that she would find a way through this situation. They explained that they too had felt this way during their lives. There were so many different varieties of hummingbirds and they each were splendid and magnificent. Some had longer beaks than others, some longer tails. Some were bigger than others. Some were more brightly coloured. What should she do?

Her daily intentions now were acceptance, loving kindness, appreciation and gratitude. Those days of confusion were over. *She could not change another's point of view, but she could change her reaction to it.* She couldn't make herself less colourful, less able to fly, less able to hover, or somersault. The day she awakened and realised these things everything changed.

This was a sacred, magical moment as the silence of the mountain, the forest, the lake and Mother Earth touched her silent receiving heart.

It was her realisation breakthrough and a truly splendid, memorable day as she understood the meaning of freedom. She now felt more whole and complete. She finally let go of being over-responsible. She now realised that she no longer needed the dis-ease to please and reflected upon how much energy it had taken from her in the past. The past was the past and she would gladly leave the old hurts and ways of thinking behind.

She was exactly who she was. Whether she had stripy wings, spotted wings, multi-coloured wings, or simply wings composed of one single colour made absolutely no difference. Her intention had not been to make others feel inadequate. She finally recognised that she was simply reflecting back to the other creatures that they too had their own beautiful qualities.

The darkest time of day was just before the dawn sun began to rise. Was the light better than the dark, or was it simply showing the contrast? Was the sun better than the moon? Was the male of any species better than the female?

The divine nectar from the flowers also reminded her of her connection to the planet itself, to Mother Earth and the simplicity of belonging and being connected to all things. Each part of this incredible jungle was joined to another. One tree provided a home for a thousand species – the insects, the birds, the butterflies, the fungi, the vines, the leaves. The branches provided a position to rest for so many creatures – the sloth, the monkeys, the snakes, the parrots and so many more creatures.

Even the roots broke through the soil to allow space for other plant species to grow. They provided a habitat for the bacteria in the soil and even the earthworms. Each and every creature had its place. Without the humble worms the soil would be like clay; without the spaces they created to hold air there would be no healthy soil. Without them there would be no vegetation and no crops. And yet so many creatures didn't like how they looked. She wondered if the worms actually cared what others thought. Did it matter anyway?

She took time to ponder the earthworms. These simple creatures who created air in the soil and in plentiful supply aided the quality of it. They sustained so many other creatures. The bigger birds loved nothing better than eating huge, juicy worms. So profound was The Wheel of Life. She had watched so many other creatures feast on them eagerly.

Her thoughts deepened with gratitude as she thought about the many beautifully coloured blossoms from which she gathered her life-giving nectar. They brought brightness into her life. Each flower seemed to bring joy into her life and she loved each one for its individuality. The orchids with their beautiful individual shapes and sizes, colours and different tasting nectars. The roses with their magnificent fragrance. The sunflowers with their amazing height and how their middles tickled her beak when she fed.

Each and every day she was grateful for her home. This magnificent jungle where the essence of connection seemed to ooze from one tree to another, from one orchid to another. Where the songs of the birds could be heard across the vast density of the other trees. The screeching howls of the monkey's laughter echoed for miles in this magical valley. What simple joy.

Chapter 6 - The Keys to Change

She had spoken to the Crow with his huge black wings compared to her tiny, light-coloured ones. She recalled a conversation they had exchanged recently. He looked sad one morning as she approached him and she asked.

“Good morning, Crow. You look sad. Are you okay. Why are you looking like that at your huge black, beautiful wings?”

“I’m sad because I have huge wings, rather than your tiny, flexible wings that have so many amazing colours,” he replied. She was astounded by his response. She allowed him to continue, listening intently to his heart-felt communication. The sadness in his voice was profound.

“I used to love my wings and now I almost hate them. I wish I was like you – colourful, bright, able to fly with such lightness, to hover, to fly backwards and to survive on the nectar from the upper valley flowers. You always have a lovely, warm smile. My wife and I know it’s so genuinely filled with unconditional love for all those you meet. You seem to be able to bring an opening, even to the tightest of closed hearts. Is it your light? Your lightness? Is it that you eat sweet nectars from each and every flower you feed from?” he continued.

“The two-leggeds reached the outer limits of the lower valley. I heard so many of the creatures crying and screaming, trying to get their families out of the way of those huge metal machines. Listening to the crunching of the tree trunks as their mighty structures were torn from the ground made so many of us weep. It was as though the trees themselves were crying out in pain.

The farmers shoo us off from their land when they plant the seeds, but now it’s the only way we can be assured of feeding our families. We get so hungry, whereas previously our life was so abundant. We always appreciated the plentiful supply. Now we realise that because we are bigger birds, we need more food than the smaller ones. It makes me feel guilty and full of shame”.

How sad she thought that he should compare himself to her. The zebras have beautiful stripes, as do the tigers. Every creature has its place. Each has their strengths and differences. It occurred to her that his pain had caused him to become confused, associating guilt and shame where once there was simply a deep peace around Crow. He loved his beloved family and his wife. She remembered watching them fly over this once untouched valley. She smiled at hearing their laughter as they raced to the top of the palm trees and crowed their mating calls which echoed beautifully through the dense jungle trees. She held love in her pure heart for this beautiful bird. She gave him time to share his truth and his feelings without judgement.

Suddenly Crow had a moment of truth. A moment of true understanding, a lightbulb awakening. The Crow realised that it wasn't simply that the Hummingbird carried joy. She was pure joy. She carried it to everyone and everything she met. She brought it to the flowers, the trees, the bees and the very air that she breathed. What a powerful thought it was.

His thoughts deepened. She carried immense gratitude and appreciation in her very essence. It simply oozed from her. The Hummingbird appreciated the flowers, the trees, the pollen, the sweetness of life and both welcomed and connected fully with everything. She was at one with all things and appreciation really was the highest vibration of all. It really was the highest form of expression.

The highest form of loving kindness to oneself is to appreciate oneself. But, he realised, anyone of us could only do that when we really appreciated ourselves in all our aspects, strengths, abilities and characteristics. What a momentous moment. Truly he was dumb-founded. He realised that he was the key to his own feelings of One-ness – the realisation that he could change his life for the better, regardless of what was happening around him.

He paused and let out a huge sigh. He had focused daily on the destruction of his beloved home. He had focused daily on the pain of all the creatures, trees, flowers and plants that had been destroyed. Yet, here he was still living. But at best, he was only living a half-life. He focused on anything that brought him sadness. He focused on listening to anyone else that talked about things that made them feel sad. Sadness had become the main subject of his conversations and even his children were now copying his behaviour.

Tears fell as he understood now how much effort it would take to change his habits, to re-educate his beloved family, returning them back to positivity. Yes, they were often hungry, yes, the farmers shouted and shooed them away, yes, the forest was being destroyed, but he still had air in his lungs and he could still choose to smell the sweetness of life. He had a choice right here and now to change. He knew he could do this.

He remembered that there were some two-leggeds who had started planting new trees. There were many who had bought land specifically which would never be destroyed. There the trees were loved, nurtured and cared for, where endangered species were being encouraged to multiply. They named it 'The Rainbow Valley'.

He realised his whole body felt lighter, the tightness in his wings had eased and the dull headache which had pained him these last few months had vanished. He was the key to his own feeling of wholeness and connection, health and well-being, regardless of whether or not the forest was being destroyed.

Crow decided to set an intention daily to seek out and focus upon appreciation. He was wise enough to know that some days it may be a struggle. He decided that he would start right now. He smiled as he realised how beautiful his wife was and how much he loved his children. He wanted to act quickly as he knew he had missed years of feeling peaceful and content. Self-peace, he thought, true self-peace.

He would start by going home and telling his wife how much he *loved and appreciated her.* Then he would tell his children how much he *loved and appreciated* them. He thought of all the various aspects of his beloved family, their quirkiness, their sense of humour, and then he realised that he even appreciated their grumpiness at times. It never lasted long. *There truly was a difference between loving someone and appreciating them, too*. His heart felt lighter and it seemed to expand in a beautiful way. He realised his wife had loved, accepted and always appreciated him.

Life would always remind him of the contrast between the light and the dark, night and the day, the Yin and the Yang. Contrast was normal, change was inevitable and every moment brought an opportunity to allow growth and appreciation. Honouring our emotions and those of others was an opportunity to learn another's point of view. It was a choice whether or not to focus on the negative, or the positive. Emotions could be observed. He no longer needed to give them control of his life. Suddenly, he had another moment of clarity. He appreciated what he had learnt from the dark cloud that had once consumed him.

Chapter 7 - The Power of Appreciation

Crow's thoughts deepened. There were both good and bad people all over the world. They were in all fields of life, in all continents. They are all part of the whole. The One-ness. *All of life was connected to The Golden Thread. It was true that there could never be separation.*

He remembered flying over the village of The Native American Indians and listening to them discuss life and wisdom. He loved to listen to their chants as they sent their appreciation daily to the Earth Mother. He had heard that throughout Mother India there were daily Puja ceremonies, celebrating Gaia.

He realised that it truly was all about appreciating everything. By appreciating our food, shelter home-life and one another, we create a natural flow of respect and harmony. With respect came more respect and therefore more connection. More respect meant deeper connections.

Suddenly, everything around him seemed lighter and brighter. He was aware of a gentle breeze against his wings, the heat of the sun and the cacophony of noises. The sound of the butterfly wings against the softness of the most beautiful petals, the most sacred orchid. He listened more intently as Butterfly kissed the petals and drank the sweet nectar. He listened to the sound of the Beetle below making his home with leaves, the sound of the Hummingbird's wings as she hovered by his side. He could hear the breath of each tree.

With a deep sadness he realised he had missed so much when he had allowed his emotional pain to consume his thoughts, cloud his mood and darken his heart. He recognised that it would have been so easy to become entrenched in even more guilt and even more shame.

He understood that he had given energy to the drama karma of life and the more he gave away, the more it had consumed him. As a consequence the more he had forgotten why he loved his beloved wife, especially her most beautiful, stunning, majestic eyes. They were like deep, tropical pools where he could get lost in his own paradise. He loved her laughter and that amazing sharp sense of humour. He recalled with sadness that she had noticed his decline into darkness and despair. She had repeatedly tried to inspire him to re-set his thinking. Now he recognised how patient she had been with him. He loved her even more. He needed to return home and share these amazing awakenings with her. He wanted to be held in her wings and welcomed home, just as it used to be.

Whilst flying home, he remembered that he could feed on the new plantations in Rainbow Valley. It wasn't much further to fly after all. Food there was in plentiful supply. It simply came down to personal choice. Was it true what Hummer had said? Did we really have the upper limits of happiness? He needed to think more deeply about this and maybe that was for another day. Was Hummer right? Could we really experience a loving relationship, health, a beautiful home and a loving family? Surely, there had to be some compromise? Could he really consider trusting in this new life? Did happiness have to have limits?

Whilst he flew, he also remembered how much energy he used to have. He was rarely tired before he had given all his power to the drama karma and the pain of life.

It was now time for change. Positive change. Now was the time to make up for lost time. Time was certainly the most precious asset he had. Hummer was right. It was about being in the present. The now truly was a magnificent gift. It was time to look forward and embrace life.

He remembered all the times he tried to make his children feel grumpy, negative, sad and angry at their plight. How he had tried to impose his feelings on everyone else around him. Everything started with him. He shook out his wings and his legs, took three deep breaths and decided to reclaim his power. The power truly was within him, just as Hummer had said. Wow, what a revelation. What a transformation this would be. No more would he waste, or undervalue his time.

As wisdom began to fill every single cell in his body, he remembered when he had first commenced this life-changing conversation with

Hummer. Wisdom, love, truth, appreciation, hope and freedom are all choices that we can consider each and every day.

Just for today, he promised himself that he would make wise choices, wise decisions. He would encourage his children to do the same. He hoped that they too would encourage others. Their wisdom could then be passed down to his grandchildren, to their children and all those who touched their lives.

"Eureka," he crowed at the top of his Crow voice.

He thought more deeply about everything. It was better to send love to those who create disharmony. Only then will they see true wisdom as their heart centres open. Their inner rose. No longer would he fear the two-leggeds, he would love them.

The Crow shrugged his shoulders and puffed out his chest as he sighed and readjusted his breathing. He loved listening to Hummingbird's wisdom and he felt something move inside his heart. It was time to open to a new way of living, a new understanding and a time to share with those who were ready to listen. He smiled a huge smile and was grateful for his beloved friend. She had clearly tried to share this wisdom for so long. He was grateful for her endless patience.

He sighed as he recognised the commitment he would need to fulfil this journey. Every day he needed to clean himself, his feathers and their home. In the same way, every day he would need to clean up his thoughts, actions, words and deeds.

"That cloud has been there for several years. It won't simply disappear. It needs to be acknowledged and worked with daily. I need to be open to understanding the lessons it has brought to me". He spoke these words with deep conviction to himself.

For the first time he understood Hummer's words when she had mentioned that he needed to become his own best friend.

Chapter 8 - Duality

The destruction of the lower valley had brought such change here. Seemingly, none of it was positive. Hummer was lost in her thoughts as she pondered if anything could be done to correct the destruction.

She considered the darkness and the dark night of the soul, the black cloud that felt like it overhung them at times. Was black a bad thing? She had always thought that black was a colour of protection, strength and retreat, a gateway to new experiences, a test of strength and resolve. Black dissolves the old to welcome in the new. Receiving Divine wisdom allows us to unearth what we have buried deep within.

She considered the Worms. They were so dismissed and unappreciated. Many people didn't even like to look at them. Yet, the health and quality of the soil could be measured by the quantity of Worms that lived in it. Surely, just as the Bees are a lifeline to living and pollenating the flowers, the Worms allowed crops to access precious nutrients and provided adequately aerated soil. She knew all creatures in life were connected. The Golden Thread was apparent everywhere she looked.

"Can you taste the sweetness of life?" asked the Hummingbird.

Hummer was reflective about her day. She felt elated that Elephant had finally trusted himself to break free of his mental chains. She was so touched to see the profound change in Crow's attitude. She remembered her spiritual teacher explaining to her that the love she had given away so freely would one day be returned to her. When that day came she would leave her beloved jungle and make her journey over the Rainbow Bridge. Her work here was completed and she was ready for her final journey home.

It was her time now. She had loved her beloved husband for many years before he was killed by the two-leggeds whilst he tried to protect their baby chicks. She cried for months, feeling lost and alone, shattered and broken. Her precious, treasured family were gone. Her beloved mate who had always made her feel so loved, so connected, so deeply appreciated and so loved died instantly. They had been together for many years. They had shared so much treasured love and a simple, yet powerful joy of just being at one with each other in a complete acceptance of one another.

She had a choice. She knew she could spend the rest of her life being sad and feeling lost. She could become angry, bitter, resentful, harsh and intolerant with all the other creatures in the jungle. Grief was a difficult emotion to swallow and experience. Yet, somehow she made a conscious choice to embrace joy. It reminded her daily of the joy she had once shared with her beloved mate. Of course there were days when the sadness seemed to engulf her, though as time went on the grief slowly eased.

Choosing to live daily, rather than exist, took energy, courage, determination and commitment.

Her time had come. As the white light from Source began to descend all around her, she breathed her last breath as she recalled the words of her soul teacher. The love she had given away had indeed been returned to her on this day. She was ready to pass over The Rainbow Bridge and be reunited with her soulmate once again. As the white light grew in strength and began to consume each of her cells, she heard the peaceful voice of her teacher repeat his favourite words of wisdom.

"Radiate Your Love."

"I am in such pain today," said the Heart to its Source.

"I have given so much love to so many I feel weary and just want to lie down and sleep."

And Source replied,

"You have misunderstood my love...I gave it to you for safe keeping and you have given it all away."

"I did not mean to give it all away," explained the Heart.

"But somehow I have, and the more of it I gave, the more they demanded."

"I am so tired. I just want to come home."

"It is *not* your time," said Source quietly.

"Learn this lesson and learn it well...for the love you have given away must return to you before you come home to me."

"Be prepared for when it returns. It will come with such force that it will smash into your chest like the bowman's arrow...to leave you bleeding, battered and torn."

"It will appear as grief, sorrow, and anguish...but it is love all the same...your love returning to you."

"What have I done wrong?" cried out the Heart.

"I have tried so hard to be loving and caring and now you tell me I am going to experience pain."

"Tell me, please, what have I done wrong?"

And Source replied, "First, let me ask you a question."

"Of course," said the Heart.

"But please be quick as I hear another knocking for my love."

"Tell me, how much of the love I gave to you have you given to *Yourself*?" asked Source.

"Very little," admitted the Heart with a sigh.

"I've always believed you wanted me to spread it into the world."

"Yes, I do," Source began to explain.

"But, if the sun gave its light away as you would have it, it would *fade and die.*"

"Then I would die also," realised the Heart.

"Exactly," said Source and smiled.

"The secret is to hold your love and *radiate* it out into the world in the same way the sun does, so that your light does not diminish."

"So, what do you need me to do?" asked the Heart.

"Connect to me now," said Source.

"Feel the power of my love."

"Wow!!!! I can feel that," said the Heart,

"It is so beautiful."

"Now hold that love in your heart...and this time we will work together," explained Source.

"OK," said the Heart.

"Together, we will create a flow of love and radiate our love out into the world in a never-ending stream."

"And whomsoever needs our love can drink from this stream."

"So go now," said Source.

"I wish you to share this teaching with anyone who will listen, help them understand this wisdom. It is so needed on your planet at this time."

"Teach them how to radiate love to create a more peaceful and loving planet...but go now because time is short."

"Can you taste the sweetness of life?"
asked the Hummingbird

Recommended Affirmation

I release myself from my past and I allow all that no longer serves me to heal, to leave my life and my physical body now. I will begin my journey to be my own best friend. I will learn to trust myself more, my intuition, my creative abilities and creative expression, my Divinity.

I promise to be kinder to myself daily. *I am that I am. I am joy. I am peace. I am respect. I am love. I am grace. I am abundance. I am one-ness.*

Each and every day I will consider this. I will make time to reflect and be silent. I will be present and in the moment. Each and every day I will consider 'The truest and most beautiful world and life that I can live is…'

'Untamed' by Glennon Doyle

Bibliography

Radiate Your Love, from Pathways to Freedom by Ken Smith. Copyright

Earth Warriors Oracle by Alana Fairchild

Untamed by Glennon Doyle

The Present by Dr Spencer Johnson

The Secret Language of Color Cards by Inna Segal

Recommended Reading

The Hidden Life of Trees by Peter Wohlleben
An Unquiet Mind by Kay Redfield Jamison
Touched With Fire by Kay Redfield Jamison
LionHearted Leadership The 13 Laws by Linda Tucker
Saving The White Lions by Linda Tucker
The Greatest Salesman in the World by Og Mandino
Who's Pulling Your Strings by Harriet Braiker
Surviving Aggressive People by Shawn T. Smith
Life Beyond the Mask by Paul Ryder
The Game by Neil Strass
Feel The Fear and Do It Anyway by Sue Jeffries
Twelve Lessons by Kate Spencer
Heal Your Life by Louise Hay
Born To Heal by Tony Hogan
Anything by Jack Kornfield
Zero Limits by Hew Len & Dr Joe Vitale
Celestine Prophecy by James Redfield
FOOD AWAKENING Nutrition for Now by Julie Silver
The Reconnection by Dr Eric Pearl
The Soul Whisperer by Anna-Louise Haigh
Light-Filled, Loving and Wise by Anna-Louise Haigh
Angel Medicine by Doreen Virtue
The Forty Rules of Love by Elif Shafak
The Shack by Wm. Paul Young
10 Mindful Minutes by Goldie Hawn
Tuesdays with Morrie by Mitch Albom
The Manuscript by Lars Muhl
Self-Care for the Self-Aware by Dave Markowitz
Light Into Life by Dr. Susan Jamieson M.D

Recommended Viewing on YouTube

Mary Curtis Healer:
https://youtube.com/channel/UCsGnB93aPLuikGA1BgCG-tA

Magic Mary's Motivational Moments and meditations:
https://youtube.com/playlist?
list=PLzAM2dy4XR0PDDRTgNNFgnVYMmTHLlaZ8

Mary Curtis Healer and interviews from my television show in 2014, *Living A Dynamic Life.*

You may also wish to look up anything by, or research the following:

- Tony Robbins
- Dan Millman
- Jim Rohn
- Dr Hew Len
- Spirit Science
- Gina Lazenby
- Emerald Tablet

Printed in Great Britain
by Amazon

56149198R00030